Advance

Memories of a Loose Woman

"Judy DiGregorio's sharp eye for life's ironies and surprises works like a magnet and the material of her essays, the humorous elements of everyday life, are drawn to her like metal filings. Judy takes a nugget of the everyday and whacks the reader's funny bone. Her stories are a delight."

—**Darnell Arnoult**, author of a novel, *Sufficient Grace*, and a book of poetry, *What Travels with Us*

"Delighted and delightful. That's how I describe the spirit singing, no, soaring through Judy Lockhart DiGregorio's new collection of essays. Whether fending off peacocks in Austria, pinch-hitting on the trombone, or saving face (and grace) onstage, she's the fierce Everywoman we long to be — brave, honest, stylish, taking aim at good intentions and foibles alike. Each essay is a glimpse of joy realized and upended, a choice slice of life, a lemon-zest punch at the end. We can't always laugh at our failings, and ourselves but we can aspire to DiGregorio's high road. We can at least follow along as she strides forth—'bold, beautiful, blazing like the bejesus in the sun.'"

—**Linda Parsons Marion**, author of *Mother Land* and *Home Fires*

"Chuckles and grins, laughs and a belly-roll here and there reside in these recollections from humorist Judy DiGregorio as she recalls the often inexplicably curious turns of day-to-day life that she has known. Judy tells of travels and adventures with the keen wit of a skilled observer whose affection for family and refuge of home connects with all of us."

—**Alex Gabbard**, author of *Return to Thunder Road* and *Gaspee*

"She's done it again! Judy DiGregorio's first volume of essays, *Life Among the Lilliputians*, tickled the funny bones of thousands of readers. Her second collection provides even more hours of delightful reading. Whether battling Velcro, dealing with the holiday panic season, or grieving over no longer being a loose woman, Judy is in her usual hilarious form. If laughter is the best medicine, *Memories of a Loose Woman*, is worth a cupboard full of pills. Good news—excerpts from both volumes will soon be available on a CD from Celtic Cat Publishing. Now we can lighten our commute or linger in our living room with the pleasant company of Judy's words."

—**Connie Jordan Green**, author of *The War at Home* and *Emmy*

"Whether confessing to her status as a 'loose' woman, ruminating on the necessity of owning a handbag 'capable of holding a Shetland pony,' or lamenting her lack of the BK chromosome, Judy DiGregorio lets sparks fly and lions roar in her newest collection of essays. Armed with double-edged wit, a razor-sharp tongue, and an unflinching eye, Judy sights down on targets familiar to most: quick fix diets, snooty cats, and those all too obvious senior moments. In this smart, witty, and irreverent collection of meditations, Judy DiGregorio scores the literary equivalent of a game-winning slam dunk."

—**Eddie Francisco**, author of *Alchemy of Words*

Memories of a Loose Woman

Memories of a Loose Woman

Judy Lockhart DiGregorio

Knoxville, Tennessee

Celtic Cat Publishing
2654 Wild Fern Lane
Knoxville, Tennessee 37931
www.celticcatpublishing.com

Manufactured in the United States of America
Interior and cover design by Greyhound Books
Front cover art by Jim Stovall
Back cover photograph by Wes Sims

We look forward to hearing from you. Please send comments about this book to the publisher at the address above. For information about special educational discounts and discounts for bulk purchases, please contact Celtic Cat Publishing.

Acknowledgement: This volume includes essays previously published in *Anderson County Visions Magazine, New Millenium Writings,* and *Senior Living.*

ISBN: 9780981923833
Library of Congress Control Number: 2010923140

For my 90-year old father, Lester L. Lockhart, who has worn many hats in his lifetime: cowboy, hobo, bus driver, Civilian Conservation Corp member, WWII veteran, career soldier in the U.S. Army, mechanic, civil servant, and family man. He remains as strong and sturdy as the live oaks of the Texas Hill Country from which he sprang.

If I get big laughs, I'm a comedian. If I get small laughs, I'm a humorist. If I get no laughs, I'm a singer.

George Burns

Contents

Acknowledgements

I could never accomplish my literary goals without the help of my husband Dan who maintains my website and my sanity, especially when technological issues challenge me. Moreover, he always laughs at my stories. I am also grateful for the support of the members of the Knoxville Writers' Guild who have encouraged and inspired me for years.

I am especially grateful to the owner of Celtic Cat Publishing, Jim Johnston, a talented poet in his own right, for the opportunity to write a second book. It is an honor to be published by a top-quality independent publisher. Thanks also to the multi-talented Jim Stovall and Cyn Mobley for their skillful work on both my books.

The Quick Fix Diet

At least once a year, something mysterious happens to my clothes. They shrink. I'm not sure why. I don't wash them in hot water. I don't dry them at high temperatures. Yet I can hardly zip up my skirts. Even my most comfortable pants, with the stretchy elastic waistbands, pinch my waist. I am not a pleasing sight, especially if viewed sideways.

As I debate the reason behind my shrinking clothing, vivid pictures suddenly flash before me — images of bottomless bowls of salsa and warm tortilla chips, thick peanut butter milkshakes, sausage biscuits with peppery gravy, and slices of pizza covered by cheese, ham, sausage, pepperoni, peppers, onions, and mushrooms. All of these images are connected with food — fattening and fantastic food. Could eating too much food possibly explain my transition from a full-bodied woman to a fat one?

I'm a lifetime member of WeightWatchers®, and strive to maintain a realistic weight. I don't want to look like Calista Flockhart. I'll be satisfied if I look like Sophia Loren. However, sometimes Krispy Kreme® doughnuts bewitch me like the sirens calling to Odysseus. I am weak, but their fragrance is strong.

When I stop following the WeightWatchers-recommended procedures of counting calories and recording what I eat each day, predictable results occur. It's amazing how a few tiny pounds can burst some great big seams.

My husband Dan works on maintaining his weight just as I do. A few years ago he complained that his clothes, too, were shrinking around the middle.

"Maybe you've just developed your abdominal muscles from all those workouts at the Fitness Club, Dan," I told him. "You don't look like you've gained weight to me."

One February morning we had to get up about 4:30 A.M. to drive our son, Chuck, to school for a band trip. The bus was leaving promptly at 5:00 A.M. For some reason, the alarm did not go off as scheduled. I woke up about 4:45 A.M. and screamed at Dan.

"We've overslept. Get dressed quick. I'll run downstairs and get Chuck up so you can drive him to school."

Half asleep, Dan rolled out of bed, grabbed a pair of jeans off the chair, and hurriedly dressed. Within ten minutes, in a frenzy to get to school before the bus departed, Dan and Chuck stumbled out the front door into the cold dark morning.

When Dan returned, I opened the front door to let him in. He waddled like a tired penguin as he came down the sidewalk. Every step, he tripped on his jeans.

"What's wrong with you, Dan?" I asked. "Why are you walking that way? Did you hurt yourself?"

"It's these jeans. Look at them. They're so tight I couldn't even zip them up this morning. It's a good thing no one stopped me for speeding or I'd have been arrested for indecent exposure. I definitely need to lose some weight."

I looked closely at Dan as he continued to take small mincing steps into the house.

"It looks like you gained some weight and lost some leg, Dan. Those jeans are dragging the ground. Is that because you couldn't pull them up all the way?"

"I don't know, but they sure are uncomfortable," Dan mumbled sullenly.

Suddenly I understood why the jeans didn't fit Dan.

"I don't think you need to lose as much weight as you think, Dan."

"What do you mean?" he grunted, sitting down on the bed.

"Those aren't your jeans. You slipped mine on by mistake. They were lying on the same chair with yours. No wonder you couldn't zip them up. We're not quite the same size or build," I said laughing.

Dan jerked off my jeans and replaced them with his own. He felt ten pounds lighter as soon as he realized he could snap them at the top.

"You don't know how lucky you are, Dan. Some of us diet for years to lose weight, but you did it just by switching jeans."

The Peacock and the Torte

A short visit to Austria several years ago with our friends, Mary and Larry, was as rich as a cup of mélange — a popular Austrian dark roast coffee mixed with real whipping cream and topped with cinnamon. We savored good food, beautiful sights, and learned about the eating habits of peacocks.

First, we traipsed the cobbled streets of Salzburg with its winding river and castle and ate in The Stiftskeller St. Peter, rumored to be Europe's oldest inn. My husband and I didn't realize that Austrian restaurants charged for bread by the slice. We merrily chomped and chewed our way through an entire basket of delicious rye, wheat, and pumpernickel bread. When the bill came, we were shocked to discover that the bread cost more than the wine and the Wiener schnitzel!

Next, we drove to a lovely spot near Weyregg am Attersee and stayed at a quiet rural inn nestled in the wildflowers and evergreens of the Austrian hills. The inn's restaurant sat on top of a cow barn, which leant a certain unmistakable ambience to the atmosphere.

At the dinner meal, the landlady escorted the four of us to a cozy wooden booth with starched linen napkins and fresh flowers on the table. A variety of colored porcelain plates adorned the paneled restaurant walls. Thankfully, we didn't even notice the smell from the barn below as we dined.

The next morning Dan and I arrived at the restaurant before Larry and Mary. I wanted to see the view from the windows on the other side of the restaurant so I sat down in a different booth. Larry and Mary had warned us that Austrian restaurant protocol differed from that in the U.S., but, of course, I'd forgotten their warning.

"We're supposed to sit in the same booth as last night," lectured Dan. "You can't just switch booths because you want to."

"Why not?" I teased.

Suddenly, the hefty proprietress charged towards us like an angry rhino, shaking her finger at me.

"Nein, nein," she grumbled, pointing toward the booth from the night before. Hastily, I jumped up and scooted across the restaurant with Dan right behind me. The landlady scolded us in German. I didn't understand what she said, but it undoubtedly meant something like "this stupid American woman can't even follow directions." From then on, I DID follow directions.

We lingered at Durnstein and the lovely Danube Valley on our way to Vienna, our last stop in Austria. In the four days we toured Vienna, we couldn't see all its wondrous attractions. The streets throbbed with Viennese men, their coats slung over one shoulder while elegant Viennese women strolled in heels and hose and fashionable dresses with beautiful silk scarves around their necks. The upscale shops and cafes on the Graben, the walking street, were easily accessible. We visited numerous cathedrals and museums.

On our last day in Vienna, we visited Kursalon, an old-style garden café in the Stadtpark, one of Vienna's beautiful city parks. As we sat outside under a green umbrella, we couldn't wait to sample the famous Viennese Sacher Torte, a rich, layered dessert of chocolate and apricot jam. An elderly Viennese woman sat down at the table next to us, laying her wooden cane on the ground. A black hat atop her sparkling white hair, she wore a matching black dress with heels and hose. Like us, she sipped her mélange and nibbled on her Sacher Torte as the orchestra in the outdoor bandstand began its afternoon concert. Soon waltzing couples began graceful sweeps around the dance floor, dipping and twirling to the Blue Danube waltz.

Several peacocks wandered in and out of the outdoor café, pecking at crumbs on the ground. One bold peacock ventured nearer and nearer our table as he flaunted his azure and emerald tail feathers and stared rudely at our desserts. Then he began to eye the torte on the table where the Viennese woman sat. She shooed him away, becoming very agitated.

"Ehr springen, ehr springen (he'll fly)," she muttered to us, as though she knew the habits of this peacock.

The bird strutted around and around her table, keeping his eyes focused on the half-eaten piece of torte resting on the gold-rimmed china plate. The woman's voice grew louder as she continued to wave her hands at the bird. Suddenly, the peacock leaped into the air and landed on the glass table, spilling coffee as he attacked the torte. The lady shrieked and beat the peacock with her purse. Wings flapping, the bird hopped down and ran a short distance away. Then he advanced toward the table again, eying the scattered crumbs.

A waiter hastened over to chase away the peacock and assist the woman. She chastised the waiter, paid her bill in a huff, and shook her cane at the bird. As she hobbled out of the café, the peacock jumped back on the table and finished the torte. We made a hasty exit before he visited our table, too.

The next day we returned to the United States, leaving Vienna with regret. We had barely glimpsed its cultural attractions in our whirlwind tour. Still, we recognized it as a city unlike any other. It offered music, history, and a Sacher Torte so delectable it transformed a peacock into a pest.

It's Only in My Head

Allergies make me sneeze,
Springtime do I dread.
There is nothing wrong with me,
It's only in my head.

The year's at the spring. My nose is in bloom. It's allergy season. I turn my face to the sun as I step onto the deck in the cool of the morning. Layers of golden pollen cover the glass picnic table as I inhale the sweet smell of hyacinth and bachelor buttons. I admire the cheerful daffodils and forsythia bushes. Then I sneeze so violently the mascara shakes off my eyelashes, and I have to blow my nose. As I continue sneezing and blowing, a pattern emerges that sounds like an Allergy Waltz, achoo, honk, honk, achoo, honk, honk. It's springtime in Tennessee when the scenery is spectacular, and so are my allergies.

I suffer from allergic rhinitis, good old hay fever. In other words, dust, animal dander, grasses, mold, and trees bother me, especially during the fall and spring. By the time the red buds pop, I'm so stopped up it feels like someone filled my ears with cotton balls. I can't taste anything, I can't hear anything, and I can't smell anything, unless it's the stinky aroma of canned sardines, that I hate, or spicy Chimayo chili from New

Mexico, that I adore. If I eat enough of this red chili, I can breathe through my nose for at least five minutes before the sense of smell deserts me again. Chimayo chili is so hot that it makes my eyes water, my tongue burn, and my head sweat, but, at least, it opens my sinuses.

It doesn't open my ears, however. When you can't hear, it's difficult to communicate effectively, as a recent conversation with my husband illustrates.

Me: Did you ask me if I wanted bratwurst?

Dan: No, I asked if you wanted breakfast.

Me: Oh.

Dan: Do you like yogurt?

Me: Sure, I think Dilbert's funny, don't you?

Dan: I didn't say Dilbert. I said yogurt. Boy, you are stopped up.

Me: What did you say?

Dan: Forget it.

My constant companions and best friends during these annoying months are antihistamines, nasal spray, and Kleenex®. Like a bluebird with nesting material, I stuff Kleenex into my purse, my pockets, and my sleeves. Instead of "Queen for a Day", it's "Kleen for a Day", or a week, or several months. One day, as I walked along the corridor at work, a friend stopped me.

"Do you have a cold?" she asked.

"Just allergies," I replied. "How did you know? My watery eyes or my cherry-red nose?"

"Neither one. The Kleenex on the back of your

leg gave me a hint," she replied. "Is that your spare?"

I gazed down and saw a neatly folded Kleenex plastered to my calf, trapped by my panty hose. I had no idea how or when it got there, but I knew I would need it before the day ended.

Yes, it takes fortitude and patience to endure the spring hay fever season. I have neither.

A Woman's Best Friend

A man's best friend is his dog, but a woman's best friend is her purse.

A purse is more than a mere accessory. It's an emergency stash, a lifeline, the fiber of our being. Purses are essential for items such as make-up, medicine, address books, calculators, cell phones, calendars, sewing kits, eyeglasses, paperback books, wallets, Blackberries, breath mints, cameras, first aid kits, gum, and hair spray. That's just the tip of the iceberg. Some women carry shoes, screwdrivers, tape measures, and even a Yorkshire terrier in their purse.

Choosing the right purse for the occasion is part of the fun. That's why women have an average of 20 – 25 purses apiece. Our inventory includes handbags such as satchels, backpacks, shoulder bags, pouches, clutch purses, cross-body purses, fanny packs, and organizer purses. We are not vain; we are practical.

For an outing with children, you need a casual bag to carry drinks, snacks, change of clothes, diapers, wipes, etc. A Sunday morning at church requires a different kind of handbag, perhaps a tasteful leather clutch or one of the huge Dooney and Burke bags carried by chic movie stars. Those bags are big enough to carry a week's worth of groceries. Then there are those special evenings at the symphony or opera when you add bling to your outfit by flaunting a sequined gold lame purse dangling from an exquisite chain.

What do women require in a purse? First, it must have a sturdy clasp to keep it closed. It also needs lots of little compartments and zippered pouches to separate the junk. Otherwise, everything sinks to the bottom of the purse, and it requires an excavation to dig up its contents. Size and shape are important, too. The purse must not be too heavy or unwieldy. We are making a fashion statement, not building up our biceps.

The other day, I did a quick inventory of my closet to determine how many purses I actually own. Among those unearthed were seven black purses, one black and white polka-dotted bag, five straw handbags, three clutch purses in red, blue, and white, one beaded handbag, one large gray bag, one lime green purse, three quilted purses in pink, blue, and turquoise, one maroon and green corduroy purse, two denim purses with wooden handles, three red purses, and one gigantic orange handbag capable of holding a Shetland pony.

My favorite purse is also the least practical one. It is a large, half-moon shaped cotton purse with black straw handles. Gaily decorated with red, green, and yellow flowers on a black background, the bag demands to be noticed. I feel like I'm in the tropics each time I carry it.

Unfortunately, no matter what kind of purse you carry, you can still have an accident with it. Some years ago, I attended a wedding at the Armstrong-Lockett

House at Crescent Bend, a lovely historical home in Knoxville. We admired the 18th century antiques and furniture of the house as we enjoyed the reception. Eventually, I paid a visit to the ladies' room to redo my lipstick. I laid my clutch purse of champagne colored brocade on the top of the commode, not noticing its uneven tilt. Suddenly I heard a splash and saw my purse floating in the toilet bowl. Quickly, I jerked it out and held it over the sink while the water drained out of it. Then I emptied the purse, wrapped it in paper towels, and feebly tried to dry it off. Finally, I rejoined the reception, but the purse dripped like a leaky faucet all afternoon and was not salvageable.

A man cannot have too many tools, and a woman cannot have too many purses.

Catalyst for Change

I use my email on the days
It works as it's supposed to.
But on the days my system's down
I wonder why I chose to.

Using email is like opening a jack-in-the-box. Sometimes it pops out, sometimes it doesn't, and sometimes it catapults to the wrong recipients with comic results. That's what happened to me when I worked for a government agency a few years ago.

For a long time, none of us had computers or email access. We handled all work correspondence through memos, phone calls, and personal visits. If someone was angry with you, he or she yelled at you over the phone or came right into your office and confronted you. Life was simple.

Then the computer age dawned, and each of us received a personal computer. I couldn't wait to use the email system to communicate with all of my friends.

The minute the email program was loaded onto our computers, our entire office stopped working in its excitement. We ignored the stacks of paper and the ringing phones on our desk as we tinkered with the email. Since we hadn't yet been trained on the email system, we learned by experimenting and sharing information. Unfortunately, we didn't share quite enough.

Composing messages was easy. Sending them was a little trickier since you had to use a pull-down distribution list and highlight the recipient's name. Gleefully, we passed messages back and forth as we explored the kinks of the system.

The first email I received was from my friend, Charlie, who sat across the hall. It read, "Judy, fix your hair." I had gotten a perm a month earlier and was badly in need of a trim. Curls of differing lengths sprouted up like dandelions all over my head. I looked like someone who had stuck her finger into a light socket.

When I received Charlie's email, I just laughed and sent back a reply saying, "Why don't you loan me a brush?" Unfortunately, when I hit the 'send' button, I inadvertently hit the global distribution list. My email traveled to hundreds of people in the building including division directors, assistant managers, and the manager himself.

Unaware of my faux pas, I continued playing with the email and composing entertaining messages for my friends, eagerly awaiting their rapid response. Suddenly, an assistant manager appeared at my door holding a large black comb in his hand with a big smile on his face.

"I don't have a brush on me, Judy, but maybe you can use this comb to fix your hair." I stared at him with open mouth as he explained he had received my message, as had everyone else in the building. Relieved he had a sense of humor, I apologized profusely.

I learned that email is neither private nor confidential. That incident sparked management to restrict the global distribution list to prevent employees from bombarding the entire office with other unnecessary emails. My errant message was the catalyst for change.

For weeks, people showed up at my door carrying combs and brushes, and my office was soon littered with them. I couldn't walk down the hall or into the ladies' room without someone reminding me of my mistake.

The mystery and magic of the email system soon faded as we learned that it had its ups and downs, like any technology. Nevertheless, we rapidly became dependent on it and used it from then on. However, no one ever again sent me a message to fix my hair.

Do-Si-Do

Swinging its head from side to side, a large black bear shuffled toward my husband, Dan. Perched on the bench of a wooden picnic table, he was blissfully unaware of the approaching visitor.

It was a crisp, cool July evening in Yellowstone National Park, and the smell of burning piñon filled the air. We had just returned to camp after a fishing trip to Yellowstone Lake where the mosquitoes were biting, but the trout weren't. We decided to play slapjack to distract our two nephews and niece from their empty fishing poles.

In our week camping out, we hadn't seen a single bear, and we eagerly looked forward to the experience. I didn't expect it to occur right at our campsite. As the bear waddled nearer, I watched mesmerized with fear, the only one at the table who noticed the bear. The others continued playing cards, intent on being the first person to slap the Jack and win the game. Finally, I unloosed my frozen jaw.

"Buh-buh-buh-bear," I stuttered, as I stood up and pointed behind Dan.

"Yeah, right," replied Dan, as he turned sideways and saw the bear about ten feet away.

"Help," he screamed and leapt from the picnic table spilling cards right and left. He gestured at us to follow him toward our green Volkswagen parked nearby. In our panic, we scattered like leaves in a windstorm, intent on getting as far away as we could from the bear. The bear completely ignored us as it sniffed around the table and found nothing to eat.

Finally, it meandered down the asphalt path towards the camp bathhouse. We followed at a safe distance. By this time, other campers had noticed the bear, and the campground sounded like the Tower of Babel as shouts and screams interrupted the quiet evening.

"Look out!"

"Bear coming down the path."

"Run!"

"Call the ranger!"

An elderly, gray-haired woman with cold cream on her face soon exited the bathhouse door. Evidently, she'd not heard our warnings. She wore a loosely tied, pink chenille bathrobe with matching fluffy slippers. Large gray metal curlers covered her head giving her an alien-like appearance. With a towel carefully draped over one arm, she daintily carried her toiletries in a pink cosmetic case.

Suddenly she and the bear were face to face. I don't know who was more surprised. The bear stood up on its hind legs and squalled; the lady threw up her arms and shrieked. The rest of us howled with laughter at the sight. The cosmetic case crashed to the ground scattering soap, toothbrush, and unused curlers. The woman's robe slid off one shoulder as the wet towel slapped her in the head. She flung the towel aside, spun around, and wobbled away as fast as she could.

The panicked bear also changed direction and galloped off the opposite way around the bathhouse. The pair met again on the other side like two square dancers. A cacophony of sounds filled the night air as the lady fled to her campsite, and the bawling bear sprinted for the woods. I doubt it returned to that campsite for some time.

After the excitement died down, we sat around the campfire savoring each detail of our adventure, including the look on Dan's face when he realized the bear was almost upon him. The bear grew larger with each telling, and we grew braver. Everyone thought it was thrilling to finally see a Yellowstone bear – especially one that could do-si-do.

'B' Words and Key Words

A ten-year old brain easily memorizes anything, but a 50-year old brain sheds data quicker than dandruff. I discovered this sobering fact during a performance of THE WOMEN at the Oak Ridge Community Playhouse.

Our director, Reggie Law, reminded us there was no need to panic if we forgot our lines. Instead, he said, concentrate on understanding the subtext beneath the lines and remembering key words.

My comic character, Lucy, sauntered into her first scene screeching "On Top of Old Smokey." Although I had the jitters the week before the show opened, opening night went well. After the show, I strutted to the car, confident the next six shows would go smoothly.

Unfortunately, fatigue overcame me during the fourth performance of the show. Though my first scene proceeded without problems, trouble lurked when I interacted with a character called the Countess de Lage. While she sipped a glass of apple juice, masquerading as bourbon, I straddled her legs, one at a time, and removed her boots. As I struggled, the Countess questioned my love life.

"Were you ever in love, Lucy?"

"Yes, Ma'am."

Her next line, "tell me about it," was the cue for my big speech, all of six lines long.

I recited the first line, recalling what a 'purty' sight it was to see my lover come 'loping across them hills.' Suddenly, the next five lines of my speech galloped away. Rocking back and forth in my boots, I remembered Reggie's advice on keywords and subtext. The letter B flashed into my mind. B, B, B. What did it mean? I squawked out the first B words that came to mind.

"Bold, bold, and beautiful." My brain hiccupped. I recalled another B word.

"Big," I said. "The sky so big and bold and beautiful." That wasn't quite correct, but I was on the right track.

I rambled on until I spit out another B word — blue. Suddenly, I realized that most of the key words in my speech started with the letter B. If I could grab on to those words, I could get the rest of my lines.

"The sky so big and blue and bold and beautiful," I repeated.

Bold and beautiful did not belong in my speech, but I couldn't stop saying those words. In desperation, I stared at the Countess. Silently, she stared back. Something about my lover's hair danced just out of reach. Brown? Black? Blond?

"Blazing," I yelped. "His hair blazing like the bejesus in the sun."

Confident I was headed in the right direction, I mentally reviewed all the B words I had mentioned

— big, blue, blazing, bejesus, and, of course, my old standbys, bold and beautiful. I needed another B word. Finally, it hit me — back fence.

"Then we'd sit on the back fence and spark," I drawled.

I'd made it to the back fence, but still needed one more keyword to propel me to the end of the ordeal. The word 'but' popped into my head.

"But, ma'am," I said, "You know how them big, strong, red-headed men are. They just got to get to the point."

With that line, I finally got to the point and to the end of my speech. Exhausted, I clumped offstage in my boots. The cast members in the dressing room overheard my speech on the monitor and were chuckling over my creativity.

"Why didn't you mention the young and the restless after you kept repeating the bold and the beautiful?" one friend asked.

"Because I only remembered words that began with the letter B," I laughed.

I had tried to follow Reggie's advice on keywords and subtext. Unfortunately, for a few minutes, I forgot both my lines AND the subtext. Thankfully, the audience didn't notice my mistakes.

Live theatre is a challenge that helps to keep the mind sharp, even if your performance is less than perfect. If I appear in another show, I don't care how big a part I get. I don't care how many lines I recite. Only one thing really matters – the keywords better begin with the letter B.

Memories of a Loose Woman

You may find this news shocking, but sometimes I'm a loose woman — especially after a visit to the chiropractor's office. It feels good to get the kinks out, but, unfortunately, the condition is temporary.

In my youth, I was as limber as a rubber band. My body bent and stretched in any direction with ease. Nothing snapped, crackled, or popped. Of course, I still had cartilage.

In college, I participated on the women's swimming, softball, volleyball, and basketball teams and kept myself in good condition year-round. Basketball proved somewhat boring since women were forced to play half-court. Forwards played on one end, and guards played on the other. As a guard, my responsibility was to grab rebounds from the opposing team, dribble to the centerline, and pass the ball to our forwards. Then I waited with the other five players, watching the game and hoping the action returned to our end of the court.

The only really exciting game we experienced during my college career occurred at the conference play-offs my junior year. It was the fourth quarter, and we were behind by two points. An aggressive forward from the visiting team elbowed and shoved me repeatedly throughout the game with no interference calls from the referee.

A stocky blond about six feet tall, she sneered at me as we jumped for one more rebound. This time she slammed her elbow against my nose. Losing all self-control, I grabbed her hair and dragged her to the floor. The fans went wild, and so did the referee. Unfortunately, he did not overlook this one infraction. Much to my coach's chagrin, he threw me out of the game. We lost the game and the championship, too. Thus ended my basketball and hair-pulling careers.

I continued to remain active and played on a coed softball team well into middle age, when I finally surrendered due to dwindling physical abilities.

First, my eyes lost their focus. No matter how hard I swung the metal bat, the ball whizzed right by me. When I did smack the ball, I ran to first base slower than a pig ambling toward a mud hole. The team hooted and yelled at me to run faster. They didn't realize I was sprinting as hard as I could in my mind, but my legs never received the message.

Out in the field, I encountered more problems. If I bent down to catch a grounder, I couldn't straighten back up to throw it in a timely fashion. Also, fly balls grew impossible to judge. I had no idea how close or far away they were and seldom caught one, although I often heard them thump the ground nearby.

When I finally resigned from the team, not one person complained. They promptly stuck someone else in right field, someone who could still bat, catch, and run.

Next I moved on to cycling. Even that proved dangerous, as I had to raise the seat incredibly high to keep from bending my knees too much. I'm surprised I didn't get a nosebleed from the altitude.

Aging presents challenges each of us must face in our own way. I accept that my days of being a loose woman are over, but I'll continue to work on my physical fitness. However, I don't support the old adage, NO PAIN, NO GAIN. My new philosophy is IF THERE'S PAIN, ABSTAIN.

Why Men Don't Change Light Bulbs

You don't need to join a fitness club to keep yourself in shape. Sometimes just changing a light bulb provides unexpected exercise options.

Our kitchen light fixture features a white globe with two sixty-watt bulbs. It's attached to a large brown fan we rarely use because of the squeaking noise it makes when it rotates. The fan has become a giant dust collector with no real purpose in life other than providing a secure base on which to attach the light globe.

Periodically, both bulbs in the fixture burn out. Since the fixture is too high to reach, we must use a chair to change the bulbs. Neither my husband Dan nor I enjoy the physical demands of this process.

A few weeks ago, I flipped the kitchen light on, and nothing happened. I pretended not to notice, hoping Dan would change the bulbs. Dan came into the kitchen and switched on the fluorescent light over the sink. He didn't even try to turn on the main fixture so obviously he knew the light bulbs were out.

After several days of waiting for Dan to change the bulbs, I gave up. I grabbed a wooden chair from the dining room table, climbed onto it, and began to remove the globe. As I unscrewed the three screws connecting it to the fan base, one screw fell onto the floor. I removed the other two, climbed down, and retrieved the mischievous screw. Then I laid all of them on the blue countertop by the sink. I cleaned the globe and set it aside to dry. Replacing both of the bulbs in the sockets, I clambered down and flipped the light switch to ensure both of them worked. I climbed up again with the globe in hand. Suddenly Dan walked into the kitchen.

"Oh, have the light bulbs burnt out? Let me help you."

"As if you didn't know," I laughed. "OK, Dan, here are the three screws. Hand them to me one at a time. Oops, sorry, I dropped one. Do you see it anywhere?" Dan bent over.

"There it is, Dan, right under the chair."

He retrieved it and said, "Let me attach the globe for you."

"Ok, hop up here. Here's the globe."

Dan positioned the globe and promptly dropped the screw. He remained on the chair as I edged around the floor.

"Here it is, Dan. No, it's a leaf. There it is. No, it's a piece of cat food. Here it is. No, it's a piece of lint. Where's that doggone screw?"

Finally, Dan jumped off the chair with the globe. As he sat it down, he spotted the screw on the blue rug in front of the sink. Back up on the chair he scrambled. I handed him the screw. He didn't drop it this time, but the holes in the globe didn't line up well with the holes in the fan base. This made it difficult for Dan to push the screw through the opening.

"I can't believe this," said Dan. "The screw won't go in."

"Let me try."

We changed places, and I successfully pushed the first screw through the hole. It dropped out immediately and successfully concealed itself on the floor.

Like a pair of old crabs, Dan, and I crawled on our knees searching for the screw. This time we couldn't find it so we gave up. Ultimately, we attached the globe with only two screws, hoping it wouldn't fall off. Two days later, we found the missing screw when I stepped on it with my bare foot. We breathed a sign of relief when all three screws were back in place in the light fixture. Later I asked Dan why most men are reluctant to change light bulbs.

"Surely, you jest," he replied. "Men don't like to change light bulbs because real men are not afraid of the dark."

A Senior and Her Moments

A new age dawns on my next birthday when I officially become a senior. Finally, I'll have an excuse for my senior moments. When I was younger, I blamed my absentmindedness on the children, my hectic schedule, or the phases of the moon. Now that I'm a mature woman, I realize there is no one to blame but myself. I lead a busy life by choice, not chance, and it makes me forgetful on occasion.

For example, once I mailed a humorous birthday card to my dear friend Thelma. Not only did she receive the first card I mailed, but she also received a duplicate card one week later. I sent her the exact same card twice so at least I was consistent and the theme was so appropriate: birthdays and memory loss.

I also often buy duplicate gifts for people. One year my mother admired a birthday book I had purchased from the Metropolitan Museum of Art. It featured a monthly perpetual calendar to keep up with important birthdays. In addition, the book included reproductions of some of the world's great artwork. Beautifully bound in an orange and green floral design, the book made a wonderful keepsake. I ordered it as a Christmas gift for my mother, and she loved it. Next Christmas I forgot I had given it to her and gave her another one!

Not only family and friends suffer through my bouts of forgetfulness. Sometimes I'm the victim. A shopping trip to a local department store last month resulted in several bargains, including a blue cotton tablecloth bordered by yellow sunflowers. When I arrived home, I admired the tablecloth again and opened the buffet drawer to store it away for later use. As I rearranged the linens, I discovered another blue tablecloth at the bottom of the drawer. It, too, sported a border of sunflowers and matched the other tablecloth perfectly. Evidently, I had snagged it at a sale at some point and didn't remember it was there.

What's even more frustrating is forgetting which DVD's I've rented when I go to the video store. Inevitably, I will choose at least one we've already seen. I've brought home "The Good Shepherd" three times, and we didn't even like the movie the first time we saw it.

Last summer we took a short trip to Lake Lure, N.C. where we admired scenic Hickory Nut Gorge, Chimney Rock, and Lake Lure. I purchased several post cards to mail to family members but didn't address them until we arrived back in Oak Ridge. I wrote a couple on the weekend, then wrote some more a few days later. As I prepared to mail the post cards, I realized two of them were addressed to my brother Charles and his wife. Both postcards featured the same lake view and the same handwritten message from me. Good things come in twos and so do postcards.

Undoubtedly, more absentminded incidents lurk

in my future, but I don't worry about them. A senior woman is entitled to her senior moments.

When Does Life Really End?

If life begins when the pets die and the children leave home, does it end when they return?

Our daughter, Candie, and ten-year old grandson, Tailen, are temporarily living with us until they move into a house. Accompanying them is a two-pound Yorkshire terrier puppy named Bone with a black pug nose framed by blond bangs. The size of a large ham hock, he is absolutely adorable and absolutely messy.

Bone refuses to eat his dry dog food pellets at his plastic doggie dish. Like a field mouse, he picks them up one at a time and stores them in different locations around the house. When you step on one barefoot, it feels as hard as a piece of Lego®.

Our two aging cats, Jewel and Colada, don't like Bone. They despise his lively moves, his yappy barks, and his high-pitched squeals. However, Bone finds the cats fascinating, especially if they're nibbling on tuna or chicken-flavored cat food. He visits their cat dish at every opportunity. If no one's looking, he grabs a piece of their dry food and sprints under the dining room table to enjoy it.

Like Bone, both cats suffer from food envy. Bone's doggie dish is a constant temptation to them, especially when it's filled with moist, bacon-flavored goop. All three of the pets suffer from water bowl envy, too. Bone prefers to lap up water from the white porcelain cat bowl. Jewel and Colada sip from his tiny water dish. The grass is always greener on the other side, and, evidently, so is the water.

Our older cat, Jewel, is on her ninth cat life. An orange and white longhaired tabby, she now needs thyroid pills twice a day. I have to keep Bone and Colada away while she chews up her liver-flavored pill, disguised in deviled ham or something tasty. In the kitchen I stand guard by Jewel while Colada, the calico, paces around meowing. Bone bounces and yips as he darts in and out my legs trying to grab the pill. The situation rapidly deteriorates.

"Eat your pill, Jewel. Hurry up. Stop, Bone. Quit barking at her. No, Colada, get away. This pill is not for you."

Soon I'm snarling like a bulldog as I shoo Bone and Colada away from Jewel and the infamous pill. In desperation, I retreat to the bathroom with Jewel, slam the door, and force the pill into her mouth. She chews it up contentedly as I lean exhausted against the door.

Other areas of the house have become chaotic, too. The garage where I once parked my silver Mazda Protégé is now crammed full of furniture and household goods. We can only reach our washer and dryer by sliding sideways and sucking in our stomach. Baskets and boxes of clothing, shoes, and detergent are piled on top of a beige couch while a blue and white comforter dangles off a chest of drawers. I trip over basketballs and bump into bicycles and bookcases trying to access the extra refrigerator where the soft drinks are stored. A metal scooter bumps my shin as I grit my teeth. To calm myself, I repeat my mantra — I do love my family, I do love my family.

This temporary relocation is not easy on Tailen and Candie either. They are unable to unpack most of their clothing or personal items because we've filled up every nook and cranny of the house with our own junk. They're forced to live out of the boxes, baskets, and bags they brought with them. With little closet space, clothes are thrown helter-skelter on top of bookcases, ironing boards, and beds.

The situation is not all bad, of course. Our daughter is a superb cook and has prepared some delicious dinners of fresh seafood and barbecue ribs. Tailen is a loving grandson and is good company, even if he is usually accompanied by several loud and boisterous friends. The house will feel empty when Candie, Tailen, and Bone move out in September. We'll miss the noise, the chaos, and the activity that youth brings. However, we'll adjust.

Does life end when the children and pets return? No, no, life doesn't end, but peace and quiet do.

From Bottom to Summitt

Some people would rather jerk out one of their teeth than speak before a live audience. Once upon a time, I felt this way, too.

Each time I had to make a presentation, my knees knocked so loudly they drowned out my quavering voice. Making any kind of eye contact with the audience intimidated me so I gawked at the note cards shaking in my hand.

I did not conquer my fear of public speaking until I worked for years at the Oak Ridge Operations Office, Department of Energy. Since my job required me to do presentations and workshops for a variety of audiences, it was imperative that I improve my speaking skills. Along with several friends, I joined Toastmasters International. Through weekly meetings, I learned to present different types of speeches. I gained confidence and ability as experienced speakers mentored and evaluated me.

Eventually, I grew more comfortable talking in front of an audience, even though I didn't always make sense. I learned to speak slowly and tell anecdotes every two to three minutes to keep people from falling asleep. I also learned to project myself with energy and to enjoy myself while giving the talk.

When my book, *Life Among the Lilliputians*, was published, my speaking career skyrocketed. I spoke to church groups, schools, civic organizations, writing groups, home demonstration clubs, retired groups, women's groups, office professionals, teachers, etc. Since I tailor my talk to each group, preparing for a speech can be time consuming. Fortunately, I save all my presentations on the computer to aid in revising and rewriting material.

Just because you're an author and a speaker doesn't mean everyone in the audience is a fan, however. At a luncheon I spoke at recently, a lady came by my table and asked if I wrote for *Anderson County Visions Magazine*.

"Yes, I do," I replied. "Do you read my column?"

"No," she said, "I only read one column in there, and it's not yours."

One of my most enjoyable recent presentations was for the Episcopal School of Knoxville. When I walked into the school, I was surprised that every student who saw me greeted me by name. The school had prepared for my visit by checking me out on Google and researching my website, www.judyjabber. com. Some of the classes wrote comments on a special webpage established for my visit. I was tickled to read one comment that began, "Dear Ms. Jabber."

The highlight of my presentations this year was an invitation to be the keynote speaker for a Knoxville medical group hosting their annual patient appreciation luncheon. Approximately 250 people were invited. I was thrilled to accept the invitation and looked forward to a prestigious speaking engagement. A few weeks later, I received an email rescinding the invitation. A well-known celebrity had just become a patient of the medical group and volunteered to be the guest speaker. It was none other than Lady Vols Basketball Coach, Pat Summitt. I was flattered to hear she was the speaker who benched me.

I don't know what the future holds for me in terms of speaking engagements, but I feel I can handle anything. After all, I've already traveled from the bottom to the Summitt.

Accessoritus Loosus

Once I was considered a well-dressed woman. Then I developed a rare condition – Accessoritus Loosus. Items such as buttons, belts, and earrings slithered, slid, and leapt from my body like children at recess. Sometimes it was amusing, sometimes disturbing, and always unexpected. The resulting effect was devastating to a woman who took pride in her appearance.

I first became aware of Accessoritus Loosus as a teenager when I strolled to church feeling quite stylish in a small white net hat with a dainty butterfly appliqué on one side. During and after the service, I preened and waited for someone to notice the hat, but no one said a word. Finally, I asked the friend next to me how she liked my hat.

"What hat? You're not wearing one," she replied.

As I trudged home after the service, I discovered the wispy little hat dangling forlornly from the branch of a redbud tree like a limp handkerchief. Retrieving it, I hastily plopped it back onto my head.

At a church service several months later, Accessoritus Loosus struck again. As I marched solemnly down the aisle with fellow choir members, someone behind me stepped on what felt like the hem of my robe and jerked me to a halt. Each time this happened, my head bobbed back and forth like a pecking chicken. The congregation tittered as I passed by, and small children pointed at me. I turned around to glare at the clumsy person following me in the procession.

To my surprise, I noticed a long red tail dragging behind me. Suddenly, I remembered the red dress I wore beneath my robe had a matching cloth belt. Evidently, Accessoritus Loosus had infected the belt. It unknotted and almost slipped away, flaunting itself shamelessly on the floor where it writhed and wriggled like some kind of belly dancer. A belt loop trapped the other end of the belt, hindering its final escape. When I reached the choir stall, I reached beneath my robe, removed the belt, and later cast it into the inner darkness of the garbage can.

Buttons are another problem for me, especially metal buttons that masquerade as plastic buttons. Everyone knows that metal buttons eat thread. It's their main diet, and they devour it like chocolate. Naturally, metal buttons do not stay attached to anything for long, even if they aren't infected with a rare condition. For this reason, I never buy an article of clothing with metal buttons, but even an experienced shopper can be fooled.

One day I dressed for work in a nautical theme, wearing a navy and white knit dress with matching Spectator pumps, polka-dotted earrings, and a thick polka-dotted bangle bracelet. The dress featured a long row of buttons down the front — yes, a long row of buttons down the front. I should have known better, but these appeared to be cloth buttons. How did I know that metal lurked beneath?

That morning, I arrived at the office without anyone handing me a loose belt, earring, or button on the way, but then Accessoritus Loosus manifested itself. First, one pierced earring popped off. I did not panic. I knew better than to search for the back of the missing earring, which had assumed a camouflage position on the floor. I just grabbed a pencil, bit off the eraser, and impaled it on the stud of the recalcitrant earring.

Taking a deep breath, I plopped down at my desk. Instantly, every button on my dress exploded into the air. The front of my dress gaped open like the Grand Canyon, but the view was not nearly so spectacular! Still, I did not surrender. Frantically searching for safety pins, straight pins, even paper clips, I attempted to fasten my dress back together. I pushed, I pinned, I prayed, but it was no use. One side of my dress drooped lower than the other, and I now resembled a large and lopsided pincushion. Accessoritus Loosus had triumphed again.

Over the years, I finally accepted my condition and learned to live with its limitations. Today I no longer wear accessories of any kind, including buttons, belts, or earrings. In fact, I no longer wear clothing. If you want to look me up, visit me at my new address - 104 Fig Leaf Drive, Mother Nature's Nudist Camp, Crossville, Tennessee.

By the way, has anyone seen my dentures?

She Lacks the BK Chromosome

A study of genetics reveals that X and Y-chromosomes determine the sex of a baby. But what about the BK chromosome? This relatively unknown chromosome determines one's ability to back up a motor vehicle. Unfortunately, it's missing from my genetic make-up.

If I'd learned to drive in a big city, perhaps I could have overcome this deficiency and developed the skill to back up a car. However, I took drivers' education classes in the small, charming village of Capitan, New Mexico. Around 6500 feet in elevation, Capitan is surrounded by the tall pine trees of Lincoln National Forest. With a population of about 500 people, the town had only two paved roads, no stop light, and no parallel parking. It did sport a caution light on the main street where travelers whizzed by the grocery store, the drugstore, and the Smokey the Bear Museum. If they blinked their eyes, they missed all these.

When we took driving lessons from a high school teacher, we drove up and down the dirt roads around town, crossing cattle guards as we headed out to the country. Occasionally, we drove on Highway 380, encountering a pickup or two. Livestock and small herds of brown and white antelope dotted the landscape as I navigated the car accompanied by a white-knuckled instructor. Driving a car scared the wits out of me and the instructor, too.

The summer I turned sixteen, I took my driving test, passing it on the first try. The test required me to drive around Capitan and then to do some maneuvers with the car, including backing it up. Luckily, I only had to back it up a few feet. Had it been further, who knows what calamity might have ensued?

During the next several years, I didn't drive the family car often, since we only had one car. On the short trips I took to the grocery store or a friend's house, I ensured the car was parked in an advantageous spot where I could just hit the gas and go forward. Thus my backing up ability never improved.

After I married, I foolishly tried to teach a friend to drive, using my own car for the lesson. Of course, the first thing I showed her was how to back up. With me sitting naively beside her, she floored the accelerator and backed all the way across a huge parking lot faster than I could say stop. She hit the one and only vehicle in the lot. I never tried to teach anyone to drive again.

My refusal to back up the van is puzzling to my children and my husband. They don't understand why rearview mirrors and side view mirrors don't solve the problem and why I circle parking lots repeatedly, searching for the perfect spot.

"Mom," said my daughter, "there's a spot right out in front of Wal-Mart."

"I can't park there, honey," I replied, driving down the next row.

"Why not?"

"Because I'll have to back out the van and someone might hit me."

If I'm driving the van with my husband as a passenger, the situation grows even tenser.

"Park here," says Dan. "We're right next to the movie theatre."

"No can do, Dan."

"For gosh sakes, don't tell me you're going to park half a mile away. We might as well walk to the movies from our house!"

"Golly, Dan, is it my fault I don't have the BK chromosome?"

I compensate for it the best I can – by not putting myself in situations where backing up is required. You have to pick the right horse for the job, and you have to pick the right spot for the car.

A Velcro-Filled Life

Santa brought me an unusual Christmas gift this year – bunion surgery. I have only one thing to say about that. Ouch! Thankfully, something beneficial came from the experience. I found some unexpected material for my writing.

After surgery, I received a black boot to wear on the injured right foot. The boot looked similar to the one I wore for my broken left foot back in October; only this boot was wider, longer, thicker, and heavier. I think it was designed for an Abominable Snowman.

My big black boot (BBB) had three Velcro strips with hook and loop fasteners. When you pressed them together, the hooks caught in the loops. When you separated them, the strips make a loud ripping (RIP) sound. This is not a suitable boot for burglars.

Taking BBB on and off each day proved to be more challenging than doing back flips on a trampoline.

As soon as I got up each morning, I placed BBB next to my right foot, grabbing Strip One that went across the top of the boot. I gently pulled the narrow 12-inch strip out of the buckle and tried to push it to the right. It waved back and forth defiantly like the tentacle of an octopus. I ignored it and reached down to undo Strips Two and Three at the bottom of the boot. RIP! RIP! Before I could finish unhooking them, Strip One attacked the hairs on my forearm. I removed it and smacked it back down. It escaped again and snagged the ace bandage around my foot causing it to unravel. The other two Velcro strips joined cheerfully in the melee forcing me to start the process all over after I rewrapped my foot.

Using both hands, I grabbed Strip One by its scrawny neck while lifting the back of my boot a short distance off the floor. I bent the strip backwards and shoved it under the boot rendering it immobile. As I picked up the hook side of Strips Two and Three with my right hand, I grabbed the loops on the left side with my left hand and attempted to heave my foot into the boot before it opened and closed like the Red Sea. Unfortunately, Strip One slipped loose again so this time I stuck it to the rug. It clung to it contentedly like a baby with a bottle. Eventually, I managed to distract all three Velcro strips long enough to actually stick my foot in the boot.

After several weeks of daily confrontations with BBB and its Velcro strips, I finally solved the problem. I found a more attractive, fuzzier target to divert the enemy. The cat hasn't forgiven me yet.

Looking for Food in All the Wrong Places

Like most married couples, Dan and I don't always agree on travel plans. I like to get on the road as daylight breaks, but Dan doesn't like to rush in the mornings. He prefers to rise at his usual time, sip two or three cups of coffee, read the newspaper, shave, and philosophize about the state of the world. In other words, he likes to ease into the day.

On a recent trip to Greenville, S.C., to see our son's new home, I tried to cajole Dan into leaving earlier by promising to stop at the first Cracker Barrel® we saw. Both of us enjoy the home-style breakfast menu. We savor the hash browns and thick country bacon along with the eggs and biscuits and gravy. With mouths watering in anticipation, we headed out of Oak Ridge with plans to stop at the Cracker Barrel near Strawberry Plains.

We sped merrily along the interstate for an hour or so when Dan suddenly looked out the window and said, "You just passed the exit to the Cracker Barrel."

"What? I didn't see any sign saying it was coming up. It's too late to turn around now. Don't worry, honey. I'll stop at the one by the Sevierville exit."

Dan looked disappointed but took it like a man. A few minutes later, we took Exit 407 heading toward Pigeon Forge. After about 10 minutes it was apparent the Cracker Barrel was not where I thought it was. Rather than waste more time, we turned around and headed back to I-40 E. As we merged into traffic, I looked up and saw a Cracker Barrel on the other side of the interstate. If I had only turned left instead of right at the exit, we would have already been smacking our lips over a tasty breakfast.

"What do you want to do now, Dan? Look for another Cracker Barrel?"

"Let's just stop at the next fast food place we see. I'm starving."

We got off at the Dandridge exit and headed toward Wendy's®. We could see its gigantic sign but couldn't find the restaurant. Finally, we figured out it was inside a tiny convenience store and gas station. Famished, we rushed to the counter to order breakfast.

"We don't serve breakfast at this Wendy's, ma'am."

"Oh, no, I guess I'll just order French fries then."

"Sorry, ma'am, but we don't open for two more hours."

Dan's face reflected the same thunderous scowl mine did as we stomped back to the van.

"I saw a McDonald's® across the street, Dan. Let's try that."

We rushed into McDonalds, grabbed a quick

breakfast, and took off again. We hadn't gone more than ten miles down the road when another Cracker Barrel sign appeared.

"I knew it," Dan said. "As soon as we stop and eat fast food, Cracker Barrels pop up like mushrooms everywhere we look."

Dan and I forgot all about Cracker Barrel as soon as we arrived at Chuck's house and saw our two sweet grandchildren, Damien and Daniele. Watching grandchildren at play is the best stress reliever there is. We returned to Oak Ridge late Sunday afternoon without even looking for a Cracker Barrel. We do plan to eat at one again soon, but this time we'll pick one closer to home. I hope we'll find it on the first try.

Answer Your Cat's Question Day

Answer Your Cat's Question Day is celebrated in January of each year. Don't be surprised if a cat looks at you quizzically on that day. This is the first year I've heard of this holiday, but it's mentioned on the internet so, of course, it must be officially sanctioned – at least by the feline community.

I have always adored cats, those warm, purring creatures that cuddle on your lap and knead you with their sharp claws. You can neither bribe nor fool a cat. Unlike dogs, they don't come when called. They just listen to the message and get back to you later. Fastidious and elegant, cats continually groom themselves to put their best paw forward. Dogs groom themselves by rolling on dead frogs, but cats have much more sense.

Many cats have owned us over the years. Thomas was a large orange tabby with a crooked tail so long that it left the room five minutes after he did. For some reason, he couldn't or wouldn't remove his tail from harm's way so someone slammed the door on it daily. His yowls could be plainly heard when this happened, but he never learned from his mistakes.

One winter night, Whitey slunk into our lives from the alley behind our stucco house in New Mexico. If ever an animal needed valium, it was this shorthaired cat. She howled so loudly at the back door we let her in just to shut her up. Twitching at every movement and sound, she performed a complete back flip every time we accidentally kicked the tin pie pan holding her cat food. Although we fed her well, she did not stay with us long.

Several years and several cats later, another orange tabby, Tang, showed up on our back porch. Long on legs and short on patience, he was the serious type. When he slept at the foot of our bed at night, he expected complete stillness. If you dared to change positions, he swatted you with his paw or nipped you on the toe. Quite often we banished Tang to another room to prevent surprise midnight attacks.

Colada, the calico, turned out to be a kleptomaniac who stole shiny objects. She was particularly fond of my costume jewelry. If I left sparkly earrings or necklaces atop the dresser, she batted them to the floor with her paw for an entertaining game of cat and jewelry. You could hear her clattering and jangling as she scampered through the house. Most of the jewelry eventually ended up in the heater vent.

My favorite feline finished out her ninth life last year. Jewel, another orange and white cat, sported soft, silky hair and a baritone voice that didn't match her heart-shaped, feminine face. Anytime I sat down at the piano to sing a song, she joined me on the piano bench, purring and meowing loudly. A longhaired cat, she preferred longhaired music and was especially fond of Italian arias.

Regrettably, we hear no patter of little furry feet in our house at present since we are cat-less. Another one has not yet adopted us so no cat will ask us questions this January. If you're among the fortunate families who own a cat, stay alert when your cat purrs and rubs against you that day. Pick it up, gaze into its luminous eyes, and truthfully answer any question it asks. No matter how long a cat lives, it never forgets, and it never stops shedding.

Finding My Niche

What do golfing and snorkeling have in common? Both can be torture if you're not skilled at them. Golfing requires a club no wider than a flamingo's leg that you use to smack a ball the size of a pea. Snorkeling demands that you wear a facemask three sizes smaller than your head and suck on a breathing tube called a snorkel – underwater, of course.

I gave up golfing after three tries because I never once achieved liftoff. My golf ball remained exactly wherever I placed it on the tee because the club and I never connected with the ball. My spirit was willing, but my swing was weak. In addition, I dug enough divots on the golf course to provide quarters for an army of groundhogs. My snorkeling attempt was only marginally more successful.

On a visit to St. John's in the Virgin Islands, we went to the underwater trail at Trunk Bay, a world famous snorkeling location. My husband Dan and my friend Mary attached their snorkeling gear with no problem. They waded into the topaz waters of the Caribbean as I vainly tried to force my size 12 feet into size six fins. I finally gave up, discarded the fins, and grabbed my snorkel and facemask.

Taking a deep breath, I pulled the mask over my head. It pinched, it pulled, and it hurt. I didn't like it one bit, and I hadn't even covered up my nose yet. Next, I inserted the snorkeling tube into my mouth as Mary and Dan demonstrated how to seal my facemask and breathe through the snorkel. To their surprise, I had no problem. Then I put my face in the water.

No matter how many attempts I made, I could not get any air through my snorkel, although I sucked in plenty of seawater. I hated having a facemask cover my nose so I repeatedly jerked it off to gasp for air. Then I had to reseal it, reattach the strap to its back, reinsert the snorkel, and plunge my face back in the water.

After about 15 minutes of this frustrating activity, I gave up completely on the snorkel and flung it under the Banyan tree along with the fins. I kept the facemask because I knew I had to use it to read the underwater signs and see the variety of coral reef life on the trail.

Mary and Dan frolicked ahead of me like middle-aged dolphins on a romp with their fins splashing merrily in my face. I could hear the excitement in their voices as they spotted purple sea fans, formations of stag horn coral, and a variety of rainbow-colored fish. I diligently swam and paddled after them at a slower pace since I lacked the advantage of fins to propel me.

Eventually, I settled into a routine as I continued my exploration of the 225-yard trail. Float face down. Look underwater. Panic. Stick head out of water like a turtle. Jerk off facemask. Gasp for air while treading water. Reattach facemask. Sink like an anchor. Kick to surface. Open mouth wide. Gulp air frantically. Look around to see if anyone noticed me. Begin routine again.

By the end of my swim, I was exhausted but proud that I'd completed the trail, even without a snorkel and fins. The adventure convinced me that I would never become a real snorkeler, any more than I would become a real golfer.

There are other sports, of course. I wonder how hard weight lifting would be?

Put Your Best Foot Forward

Though I've endured my share of accidents over the years, I never broke a bone until last month.

In my youth I lived on Guam, Marianas Islands, and in the Panama Canal Zone where playing Tarzan was a popular activity. I often fell out of trees, usually after grabbing a rotten branch. Other accidents resulted from doing daredevil tricks on my bicycle, although none resulted in serious injury, except to my dignity.

When I moved to New Mexico during high school, I learned to ride a horse. Unfortunately, I spent more time on the ground than on the horse because my good friend, Judy M., wanted me to learn to ride bareback like her. Every time her horse Spook threw me off, she cajoled me into getting back on. I don't know if I was brave or stupid, but I spent a lot of time sitting among prickly pears. I never did evolve into much of a horsewoman, but I took some hair-raising rides.

After checking the mailbox one day last month, I began to skim through a copy of "Architectural Digest" and paid no attention to where I was walking. I accidentally stepped off the high edge of our asphalt driveway, twisting my left foot in the process. It struck the ground forcefully, and I gave a yelp of pain. I leaned on the car for a few minutes, mumbling and moaning to myself. Then I gathered up the mail I had spilled on the ground and hobbled into the house.

Since I thought I had only sprained my foot, I didn't go to the doctor, assuming the foot would soon heal by itself. By suppertime, my foot had swollen up some, but the pain wasn't that bad. I didn't even take a Tylenol®. It wasn't until the next day that I noticed my foot had turned a lovely shade of purple. The color complemented the two toes that had turned black and blue. The injury didn't slow me down that much, although it was painful to squeeze my fat foot into a shoe. After two weeks, I was surprised to see a huge knot appear on the side of my foot.

A visit to the doctor's office confirmed that I had not sprained my foot but broken a bone. As a reward I received an ugly fracture shoe made of denim. I'm a vain woman who likes to coordinate her accessories, but nothing in my wardrobe matched the shoe except for a pair of jeans.

My friend Betsy insisted I come by her house so she could brighten up the dull shoe to make it more appealing. She did a fantastic job of gluing on baubles, bangles, and beads of all colors and sizes. She even added my initials in gold on the back. The fracture shoe became a work of art and sparkled like a queen's tiara. It flattered any outfit I wore. Everywhere I went people admired it.

Sometimes you don't put your best foot forward, you put the worst one. But you do it in a dazzling shoe.

And the Band Played On

When you attend a fifth grade band concert, you don't expect to hear a skilled performance. Beginning instrumentalists generally shriek and squawk like blue jays. However, Dale Pendley, Jefferson Middle School Band Director, from Oak Ridge, Tennessee, is an experienced director who knows how to get the best sound from his students. He uses innovative ideas to motivate them to practice such as scheduling an annual parent band concert. By teaching parents to play their instrument, student skills are reinforced, and parent skills, or the lack of them, are exposed for the entire world to hear.

Because Tailen's mother had no time to practice with him for the concert, he begged me to participate instead.

"Please, Grandma." Tailen's brown eyes welled up, and my resolve melted like a Hershey bar as I reluctantly agreed.

Tailen opened the velvet-lined black trombone case and showed me the basics of assembling the trombone, including how to empty the spit valve. He demonstrated how to hold the trombone, blow into the mouthpiece, and move the slide. Then he showed me some exercises to loosen my lips.

Next, he retrieved his *Essential Elements Band Book* and played the first tune, "Rolling Along," also known as "Mary Had a Little Lamb." Now it was my turn. When I blew into the mouthpiece, it sounded like a cow bellowing in pain. Mary's little lamb was doomed to become Mary's big lamb before I mastered the song.

Tailen's patience soon ran out, and we only practiced two more times before the concert. On the Thursday before the big night, Tailen brought home a note from Mr. Pendley that listed twenty songs parents should be prepared to play during the concert. I had learned to play only three notes, G, F, and C, and hadn't even conquered one song. Twenty songs? I began to hyperventilate.

The Tuesday night of the concert, I entered the cafeteria of the high school with Tailen and discovered only a few parents were actually participating in the parent band. Most of the group had played in high school or college bands and were experienced musicians, although a bit rusty. The parent band included three men on trumpet, two women on clarinet, and one woman on percussion. I was the only trombonist. There was no way to hide in this small crowd.

By now Tailen was as nervous about my performance as I was. He wouldn't even pass me his trombone so I could warm up.

"You don't play it right, Grandma. I don't want my friends to hear you."

"Too bad, Tailen. Mr. Pendley is counting on my

playing with the parents, and I'm going to do my best. Hand over that trombone."

Like a flock of sheep, we followed Mr. Pendley on stage. The parent band sat down on metal chairs in a semicircle on the front row with the student performers behind us. Several hundred spectators stared back at us from the auditorium. Please, God, let everyone drown me out, I prayed.

Mr. Pendley waited as we placed the band books on our music stands. Then he announced the song and page number, raised his baton, and we were off. I stayed off the whole time like a racehorse that never left the gate. I blew and tooted the trombone every time I saw the notes G, F, and C. The rest of the time, I faked it and moved the slide up and down. Sweat trickled down my back as we ran through our repertoire and finished with our finale, "Lean on Me." By then, I was more than ready to lean on someone. Except for my discordant notes, the parent band sounded quite good.

Relieved the ordeal had ended, I handed Tailen's trombone back to him for the student band performance.

"Grandma," he whispered, "you weren't moving the slide at the right time."

I patted him on the shoulder, knowing my performance had been a disappointment. As I walked to my seat, several people complimented me on my playing, and one even invited me to play in a brass quintet. Obviously, I had fooled some people, but I knew I hadn't fooled Mr. Pendley, and I certainly hadn't fooled Tailen.

For my grandson's sake, I had attempted to conquer the mighty trombone. The trombone won.

Metamorphosing into Mrs. Magoo

Mr. Magoo, the near-sighted cartoon character, was one of my favorites in my youth. Watching him stumble and bumble around without his glasses caused me to howl with laughter. Of course, I had excellent eyesight then and couldn't identify with anyone who didn't. This changed when I reached middle age and discovered I could no longer read the newspaper. I needed the long arms of an orangutan to position it at the right distance.

A visit to the eye doctor confirmed my suspicions, and I purchased my first pair of glasses. Avoiding the high-priced designer lenses like Armani and Gucci, I chose a moderately priced frame of bright red for my lenses. The glasses flattered my face, and I wore them proudly for a short time. Then they became somewhat of a nuisance, and I wore them only when I really had to.

Like Mr. Magoo, I encountered problems without my glasses. I often misread my emails, including the one I received from someone named Arm Pit. When I put my glasses on, I realized the first name was Ann instead of Arm.

Another incident happened with my son, Chuck, who is fond of motorcycles. He likes to race them, paint them, and build them. One day I was surprised to see him in a tee shirt that sported a religious slogan about cyclists.

"Chuck," I said. "I've never seen you wear a shirt like that before."

"What are you talking about, Mom?"

"The slogan on your tee shirt says 'Jesus Saves Choppers.'"

"Put your glasses on, Mom. It says 'Jesse James Choppers.' That's just a brand name."

Even at church, I made embarrassing mistakes when I didn't wear my glasses. In an effort to be friendly during the coffee hour, I introduced myself to a redheaded woman whom I didn't recognize. Her response startled me.

"For heaven's sake," she said. "This is the third time in the past couple of months you've introduced yourself to me. Can't you remember who I am?"

Horrified, I stared open-mouthed at her as my brain worked furiously to identify the strident lady.

Finally, I said, "I'm sorry I didn't remember you, but you've changed your hair-do and your hair color, haven't you?" Indeed she had, not once but twice in the past months. Her own mother wouldn't have recognized her, even if she WERE wearing her glasses.

The other day I rode the bicycle at the gym while waiting for my husband to finish exercising on a nearby machine. Though I could only see his back, I recognized his white hair, grey tee shirt, and tan shorts. Each time

I thought he was finished, he bent over and started the routine all over again. Suddenly my cell phone rang.

"Where are you?" asked Dan.

"Watching you work up a sweat," I replied.

"I don't see you anywhere."

"Well, turn around. I'm on the recumbent bike right behind you."

"There's no recumbent bike behind me. I'm waiting for you downstairs in the lobby."

"Really? OK, I'll be down in a minute." Sashaying by Dan's look-alike, I realized I didn't know the man at all. I was glad I hadn't sneaked up behind him and done something stupid like pinching his biceps.

These days I wear my glasses because I can't read the microscopic prices on food items at the grocery store, at the drug store, or at the department store. In addition, putting on make-up is riskier than it used to be so I have to ensure I've applied lipstick on my lips and not my chin. I have finally accepted the fact that I must wear glasses. Not only do they help me see better, but also they're quite effective at camouflaging wrinkles.

Surviving Home Repair and Remodeling

Before couples marry, they ought to test their relationship to see how strong it is. One way to accomplish this is to complete a repair or remodeling project together. The couple who survives this can usually survive the challenges of marriage.

The first home repair adventure Dan and I experienced occurred at a one- bath, three-bedroom, wood frame house. The old commode in the bathroom leaked constantly. Finally, one Saturday afternoon, Dan decided to surprise me and fix it.

He lifted off the toilet lid as the water inside hiccupped and gurgled, but he saw nothing wrong. Then he noticed the bottom of the commode was cracked and the wax ring sealing the commode had deteriorated. These problems explained the puddle of water in the bathroom each day.

Dan knew what had to be done. He had to replace the old commode with a new one. Like the old "Rawhide" song, he headed up the toilet and moved it out. Unfortunately, most of the rotted bathroom floor came with it, leaving a gaping cavity exposing the ground below.

I stood in the kitchen madly mixing up lasagna and making appetizers for the ten people we had invited to dinner that night. Somehow, this occasion had slipped Dan's mind. He peered in the kitchen door, described the catastrophe in the bathroom, and told me he was on his way to buy a new commode. Dan was shocked at my angry reaction to his news.

"But you wanted me to fix it," he kept repeating.

"Yes, yes, I did," I sputtered, "but not on the day of our dinner party!"

Now there was no toilet, no bathroom floor, and, if I could have caught Dan before he sprinted to the Volkswagen, there would have been no husband. He returned home shortly with a pristine white commode and several boards to temporarily cover up the missing floor in the bathroom. Working feverishly, he managed to install the commode before the first party guest arrived. The dinner party was saved, and so was Dan's neck.

Nine years later, we moved to a basement rancher, surrounded by pink dogwood trees and a towering magnolia in the front yard. The kitchen in the new place didn't have enough cabinets so Dan decided to hire a fellow teacher named Bill to remodel the kitchen.

Bill's expertise in home repair and remodeling was legendary. He started on the kitchen, gutting the cabinets and tearing down walls after we disconnected the stove and moved the dishes and pantry stuff into the living room. Before Bill could finish that project, Dan tasked him to fix the shower in the master bedroom that was leaking into the basement. The bathroom floor under the shower needed to be removed and replaced so this was a major chore, but at least we had a second bathroom to use.

While Bill began work on those two projects, Dan decided that our ceilings needed to be touched up and repainted. A stepladder, drop cloths, and buckets of paint materialized, and the house began to resemble an obstacle course.

Bill worked hard on all of the projects Dan gave him, but in addition to being a full time teacher, Bill coached a middle school football team, so he had to squeeze in our projects when he could. Sometimes days or weeks would pass before we saw him.

Over the next several months, Bill spent so much time at our house that he became one of the family, just like Eldon, the painter, on the old Murphy Brown television series. Sometimes Bill appeared at our house at seven in the morning. Other times he showed up at nine at night. We welcomed him at any hour.

After a while I grew very weary of smelling fresh paint and inhaling sawdust. I longed to cook a meal in my kitchen again. Thank heaven, Dan finally ran out of chores for Bill, and Bill finished all of the projects. He repaired the shower and bathroom floor, painted all of the ceilings, installed new kitchen counters and light fixtures, and hung the new kitchen cabinets. Oak stained cabinets with glass panes now displayed our dishes, and blue tile countertops contrasted nicely with the yellow kitchen walls. The projects had taken a long time due to Bill's high standards and busy workload, but the end result was certainly worth it.

Though tempers flared from time to time, Dan and I learned that we could endure the chaos and discomfort inherent in home improvements. Home repair and remodeling do not have to end in remarrying.

A Woman's Favorite Invention

Aman is thankful for the turkey on Thanksgiving, and the gravy and mashed potatoes, too, but a woman gives thanks for much more than that. She offers thanks for that wonderful invention that permits females to truly be themselves, that allows them to bend and stretch and expand. Yes, I mean elastic, the essential element in every woman's waistband, especially after a big Thanksgiving meal.

Who invented elastic? Who cares? The important thing is that its creation saves women from zippers that refuse to zip and buttons that explode when you fasten them because they can't contain the voluptuous flesh of a real woman. Most women are not like the 'stick' women who model for *Vogue*® magazine. Those women weigh less than a number two pencil and cast no shadow on the sunniest day.

Neanderthal women didn't worry about a small waistline or a svelte figure. Outrunning a cave bear or other prehistoric beast was more of a priority. Clothed in animal pelts, they lived free from fashion or figure constraints. If they ate too much, they used their own version of elastic, a piece of rawhide or animal gut that held the pelts on their body. When they needed more breathing room, they just loosened the rawhide or gut, allowing their bellies to hang out. This is how the saying developed — to spill your guts.

What did Neanderthal women prepare for Thanksgiving? Perhaps they celebrated with a bison brunch or a wooly rhino roast without the wooly. Reindeer and waterfowl were also plentiful and would have provided quite a feast, especially if served with scorched rabbit on the side.

As delicious as a Neanderthal Thanksgiving sounds, it doesn't quite appeal to my taste. I prefer an old-fashioned meal cooked on a stove, instead of a campfire. However, like Neanderthal women, I do a little hunting and gathering before the big day. I hunt a 20-lb turkey at the supermarket that will feed six to eight people. I gather the groceries to make the broccoli casserole, the mashed potatoes, the cranberry relish, the pecan and pumpkin pies, and the fragrant yeast rolls like my mother always made.

On Thanksgiving morning, we pop the turkey into the oven as early as we can so we can gobble it up as soon as possible. Once the bird starts to cook, we open the oven door frequently to inhale the delicious aroma and check on the status of the turkey. This is the most difficult part of Thanksgiving, waiting for that magical moment when the golden brown turkey is pronounced done by my husband, the official turkey roaster.

Each year I vow not to overeat at the meal, but I lie. Again and again, I fill my plate, savoring each delicious taste. I give thanks for family, friends, and food, and that special something around my waistline that allows me to enjoy all of it – elastic.

Words Better than Chocolate

Some years I am satisfied with a box of Russell Stover chocolates for Valentines. Other times I crave something more substantial. This year I treated myself to the gift of a poetry-writing workshop sponsored by the Tennessee Mountain Writers.

Stop rolling your eyes. Workshops are great fun. Yes, you sit around a table for hours discussing the meaning and nuances of words, but you meet interesting, creative people. You savor wonderful stories and poems. You share your successes and failures with other writers who do not judge you. In addition, you are usually inspired to write some new material.

I realize some people prefer chocolate to words. Words have no smell or taste, but they can still fill you up. There's nothing more fulfilling than playing with a group of words and watching it transform into a poem or a story. And if someone publishes your words, it can make you almost drunk with excitement.

My mother introduced me to the beauty of language when I was quite young by reading me Mother Goose rhymes, including my favorite:

The North Wind doth blow
And we shall have snow
And what will poor robin do then, poor thing?
He'll sit in a barn and keep himself warm
And hide his head under his wing, poor thing.

Granted, this verse is commonplace and predictable, but yet it stirred something in me. I repeated the words for years, although my mother probably prayed I would forget them.

I began writing rhymes in second or third grade and graduated to limericks and light verse in high school. In my view, these do not fall into the same category as poetry. Poetry uses imagery, metaphor, and rhythm. As Dana Goia says, "Poetry is the art of using words charged with their utmost meaning." My humorous verse does not accomplish all of this, but I still enjoy writing rhymes such as the following:

If you write in iambic pentameter,
Don't worry about the parameter.
Just count one to five,
There's no need to jive,
We'll know that you are no amateur.

I admire true poets such as George Scarbrough and Pablo Neruda with all my being and I hope one day to write a real poem. However, like fine wines, some talents take a long time to age. My poetic talent is still fermenting in the barrel.

I'd rather be clever than dumb,
But the wit that I seek just won't come;
I think and I think
Till I feel on the brink,
But the words that pop out are 'ho hum.'

Double Trouble: A Story of Two Rascals

A perky new neighbor has moved in next door. His name is Roscoe. A six-month old Yorkshire terrier with a tan and black coat, he is playful and energetic. His eyes sparkle with intelligence while his tail wags constantly. Roscoe is quite gregarious and barks a greeting anytime he sees us. If he's not on his leash, he quickly dashes over to greet us in person. He'll lick your face as long as you let him. We treasure his surprise visits, although we discourage him from leaving his yard without one of his owners, Joy and P.J.

Generally, Roscoe is on a leash so he can't run away, but occasionally his owners try giving him a little freedom in his back yard. However, Roscoe can't resist exploring other yards, too. The other day, Dan and I stood on our back deck and saw a ball of black fur sprint by below.

"There goes Roscoe," said Dan laughing. "P.J. won't be far behind."

Sure enough, P.J. soon ran across the yard after the dog. Each time he got close to Roscoe, the dog dashed off in another direction. Twisting and turning like a quarterback, he out-maneuvered his captor and flopped down on the grass for a short rest. P.J. did his best to lure him back home with a toy. Roscoe followed for a short time but then bounced off to investigate a rotting banana peel.

It took about twenty minutes to capture the mischievous puppy. As P.J. carried him home, Roscoe looked up at us and barked as if to say, "Don't worry. I'll visit you tomorrow." Dan and I couldn't help laughing at Roscoe's antics. Like most Yorkies, he has a will of his own. Perhaps his name should be Rascal instead of Roscoe.

We first became acquainted with Yorkies when our daughter bought a miniature Yorkie three years ago. My grandson named him Bone because of his tiny size. We fell madly in love with Bone and enjoy his cocky personality. Like Roscoe, however, Bone, has a mind of his own.

If you mention the word 'walk,' Bone spins in excited circles. He loves to go to the Oak Ridge Marina and yips and yelps as he waits for me to release him from the car. I don't dare do that without the leash attached to his collar. Then Bone pulls me down the path barking at the geese and checking out the trashcans. Unfortunately, after about 100 yards, he stops, turns around, and faces the direction of the car. No matter how much I cajole or beg him, he will not walk another step unless we move toward the car.

Exasperated, I finally pick him up and cradle him in my arms, supporting his tiny feet with one hand.

We continue down the trail toward Flatwater Grille. Bone and I enjoy the fall foliage as I walk and he rides. Even though he only weighs five pounds, he gets heavy. Every five minutes or so, I set him down to see if I can persuade him to finish the walk. Stubbornly, he turns around backwards and faces the parking lot again. We repeat this routine over and over until we finally reach the wooden bridge near the restaurant.

Bone knows this is where I turn around and head back toward the car so he allows me to set him back down without complaint. Holding his head and ears erect, Bone is now all business. Finally pointed in the direction he wants to go, his little feet tap rapidly on the asphalt as he stops to sniff trees and bushes. We're back at the car in record time, but, as usual, I have gotten far more exercise than Bone.

Yorkies are independent, intelligent, and irresistible. I have only one bit of advice for Yorkie owners. If you can't train your Yorkie to do what you want, don't worry. He'll train you.

More than Four Seasons

Years ago, Copernicus discovered the sun was the center of our solar system, thus unraveling the science of the seasons. What he failed to realize, however, was that the fall equinox signals the beginning of another important season — the holiday panic season.

As the sun's rays grow weaker and winter's chill drifts down upon us, the specter of future holiday chores floats before me. The days grow shorter. There is less time to plan, less time to shop, yet more time to panic.

At first, the panic is as subdued as the chirping of a cricket. I successfully push it aside through October while I'm distracted by Halloween. Then it's November, and I'm distracted by the Thanksgiving holiday that sneaks up on me like a cat on a bird.

I make my plans for the Thanksgiving meal: buy the turkey and the trimmings, bake the pumpkin and pecan pies, make the mashed potatoes, green bean casserole, and cornbread stuffing, buy Alka Seltzer for after the big feast, and remind myself to turn on the oven.

One year, my husband Dan stuffed the turkey, plopped it in the oven, and we went for an early walk in the crisp November air. We were surprised that the house didn't smell like roasting turkey when we returned. Dan checked the oven temperature and made an important discovery. No one had turned it on. Our meal was a little later than planned that day.

The Friday after Thanksgiving is the official opening day of the Christmas shopping season. By now, my panic has swollen to the size of a hot air balloon as I, like countless other shoppers, realize there's only one month left to shop for Christmas.

I need a little shopping list. No, I need a big list. Unfortunately, each list I scribble slips away like a ferret and hides in the bottom of my pocketbook or under the pile of reminders and writing magazines on my dresser.

My Franklin planner-type friends don't suffer from my lack of organization. They have completed their tidy little Christmas lists and shopping before I've even charged my first gift. Some of them bought this year's Christmas gifts at last year's after Christmas sales. Really, they are disgusting. It's not sporting to shop so far in advance.

It's much more challenging to wait until the last minute and dash madly from store to store on Christmas Eve searching for the digital camera your husband requested or a Game Boy cartridge for your grandson. Though store inventory decreases, there are many bargains available – if you can stand the pressure.

Only once did I actually manage to buy Christmas gifts early. With a mail order catalog in hand, I circled cheese and sausage, Christmas stollen, flavored coffees, and other food items to send to out of town relatives. I phoned in the order on October 30.

"Remember," I advised the salesclerk, "this is a Christmas order, not a Thanksgiving order. Don't ship any of these items before Dec. 10 or so."

I marked off 'out-of-town' gifts on my list, grateful that at least one holiday task was done. I didn't discover until after Christmas that none of the gifts I ordered was delivered. I chatted with my sister Mary to see if she had received the sweet rolls and the tin of spiced pecans we sent her.

"No, we didn't get anything from you this year," she responded. "Neither did anyone else in the family."

Aghast, I phoned the mail order company. They informed me that their computer crashed in November and deleted all the order information. Since they had no hard copy records of who had ordered what, they only shipped new orders that came in after the computer was repaired. The one year I was organized enough to order gifts in advance, a computer snafu sabotaged my efforts.

It's already November, and I have two more months of panic to endure before I make it through the holidays. After that, I won't suffer another panic attack for quite a while, probably not until the spring equinox in March. Then my thoughts turn to warm weather and summer vacations and beaches. Beaches mean bathing suits. I gulp at the thought of it. That's how the bathing suit panic season begins.

Lights Out in Kiawah

W hy did you bring me to a place with live alligators, Grandma?" asked my six-year old grandson. It was our first visit to Kiawah, South Carolina, a barrier island with a world-renowned golf and tennis resort.

"Because I didn't know alligators lived here," I replied.

In fact, I was quite uneasy to see alligators paddling through the muddy lagoon outside our condo's screened porch. I knew Kiawah was a five-star resort for tourists. I hadn't realized it was a five-star resort for gators.

Kiawah is a perfect spot for a family vacation because it offers a variety of activities from nature talks and tours to golfing, tennis, and bike riding. The lush island with its semi-tropical climate features numerous bike trails plus an ample beach that beckons you to skim across it on your bike in the morning and inhale the fresh sea air. You can also observe the sea life that washes ashore: horseshoe crabs, starfish, and countless pink and white jellyfish that look like sushi.

The first year we rented bicycles at Kiawah, both Dan and I were a little clumsy on them. We hadn't ridden bikes in years. We lurched and swayed trying to balance ourselves like someone with an inner ear infection. Of course, one of our rental bikes was a tandem to allow us to carry Tailen on its back seat. We didn't quite trust his navigational ability around lagoons teeming with gators.

The Kiawah cruising bikes were sturdy, one-speed bikes with wide, comfortable black leather seats. They had wide handlebars and foot brakes. However, I kept forgetting about the foot brakes so I squeezed the non-existent brake on the handlebar instead. This resulted in several 'hit and curse' accidents. I did the hitting, usually running into the back tire of Dan's tandem bike. Dan did the cursing as he wobbled down the path with Tailen leaning right and left on the rear seat. They only crashed once or twice and usually landed in a stand of palmetto trees. I don't understand why they blamed me.

After several visits to Kiawah, our bike riding has steadily improved. Now we enthusiastically glide down the paths lined with magnolia trees and moss-draped live oaks. We watch furry voles dash in and out of magenta hibiscus blooms and scarlet calla lilies. No matter where we pedal, we pass a picturesque golf course or pristine lagoon, usually with stiff-legged herons or cranes gobbling up their daily quota of fish.

We always visit the Kiawah Nature Center, too. The staff naturalists provide talks and tours that discuss the island birds, sea turtles, snakes, and gators. After one evening excursion by van, we arrived back at the Nature Center about 9:30 P.M. The tour instructions directed us to bring flashlights, but we had forgotten them. They weren't necessary on the tour anyway.

As soon as we left the Night Heron Park area, we realized why the Nature Center staff had told us to bring flashlights. There were no streetlights in the direction of our condo because of restrictions that protect the loggerhead sea turtles that lay their eggs on the Kiawah beaches.

The adults and hatchlings find their way to the ocean by following the moonlight reflecting off the water. To avoid confusing the turtles, everyone is asked to turn off all lights that can be seen from the beach. The lack of artificial light benefits the turtles but didn't help us at all.

Even Tailen's young eyes couldn't see through the inky blackness that surrounded us. Hands clasped together, we decided to avoid our usual path home that passed two lagoons. The thought of accidentally stepping on an alligator in the dark made us nervous.

Like the Three Stooges, we plunged forward onto an asphalt path that headed for Mariner's Watch, our residential area. Unfortunately, we couldn't tell the street from the curb or the sidewalk from the grass.

Our conversation, punctuated by screams and yells as we tripped and fell over unknown objects, sounded like this:

Dan: Gosh-a-mighty, it's so dark out here I can't even see my own feet.

Tailen: I hear something crawling in the bushes, Grandma.

Me: I can't believe we didn't bring any flashlights.

Dan: Is that a log over there or a gator?

Tailen: I don't want to be eaten by an alligator!

Me: Something just ran across my foot.

Dan: Where the heck is the path to our condo?

Tailen: Are we lost?

After a slow and tortuous trek, we stumbled our way back to our condo. Dan, with arms outstretched, led us Frankenstein-style, to avoid hitting trees and bushes. Tailen and I clung to his shirttail praying for deliverance. Finally, a few dim porch lights enabled us to recognize our red van and find our condo. Gratefully, we staggered up the stairs and collapsed inside on the flowered sofa.

It was a night we'd never forget. Neither would we ever again forget our flashlights.

About the Author

Judy Lockhart DiGregorio is an Army brat from San Antonio, Texas, who has lived in Oak Ridge, TN, since 1969. She is a retired training specialist from the Oak Ridge Operations Office, Department of Energy. She's now a freelance writer whose writing is included in numerous anthologies and other publications including the *Chicken Soup* books, *The Writer*, and *The Army Times*.

Judy is currently humor columnist for *Anderson County Visions Magazine* and helps write press releases for the Oak Ridge Community Playhouse where she frequently appears on stage. Celtic Cat Publishing published Judy's first collection of humorous essays, *Life Among the Lilliputians*, in 2008. The book was featured at the 2009 Southern Festival of Books in Nashville, TN.

In her spare time, Judy is a charter member of the Steering Committee for Girls, Inc., serves as President of the Oak Ridge High School Track Boosters Club, and serves on the Knoxville Writers' Guild Board of Directors. She also sings with Varying Degrees, a women's singing group that entertains with eclectic music. Judy's favorite hobby is spending time with her three grandchildren, Tailen, Damien, and Daniele. She's married to Dan DiGregorio, her first and last husband.

Visit Judy's website and blog at http://judyjabber. com.

About Celtic Cat Publishing

Celtic Cat Publishing was founded in 1995 to publish emerging and established writers.

The following works are available from Celtic Cat Publishing at www.celticcatpublishing.com, from Amazon.com and from major bookstores.

Poetry

Exile: Poems of an Irish Immigrant, James B. Johnston

Marginal Notes, Frank Jamison

Rough Ascension and Other Poems of Science, Arthur J. Stewart

Bushido: The Virtues of Rei and Makoto, Arthur J. Stewart

Ebbing & Flowing Springs: New and Selected Poems and Prose (1976-2001), Jeff Daniel Marion

Gathering Stones, KB Ballentine

Fragments of Light, KB Ballentine

Guardians, Laura Still

Humor

Chanukah

Breinigsville, PA USA
24 May 2010
238578BV00002B/5/P

9 780981 923833